AMERICA'S FIRST HIGHWAY

Greg Roza

The Rosen Publishing Group's

PowerKids Press™

New York

Published in 2009 by The Rosen Publishing Group, Inc.
29 East 21st Street, New York, NY 10010

Book Design: Daniel Hosek

Photo Credits: Cover, pp. 8, 12, 13 (bottom), 14–15, 16, 17, 20, 21, 22, 23, 24–25 courtesy of the
Lincoln Highway Digital Image Collection, Transportation History Collection, Special Collections Library,
University of Michigan; p. 4 © Ron Chapple/Corbis; p. 5 (top) © Anna Dzondzua/Shutterstock; p. 5 (bottom)
© Tim Graham Photo Library/Getty Images; p. 6 © Michael Maslan Historic Photographs/Corbis; p. 7 ©
PEMCO-Webster & Stevens Collection, Museum of History and Industry, Seattle/Corbis; p. 9 © Streeter Lecka/
Getty Images; p. 11 (top) © Underwood & Underwood/Corbis; pp. 11 (bottom), 26 © Corbis; p. 13 (top) ©
Keystone/Hulton Archive/Getty Images; pp. 18–19 courtesy of The Lincoln Highway National Museum & Archives
(www.lincoln-highway-museum.org); p. 28 courtesy Library of Congress, Prints and Photographs Division.

The Rosen Publishing Group would like to thank Kathleen Dow, curator of the Transportation History Collection
at the University of Michigan, for her help in obtaining images for this book.

Library of Congress Cataloging-in-Publication Data

Roza, Greg.
  America's first highway / Greg Roza.
      p. cm.
  Includes index.
  ISBN 978-1-4358-0199-8 (pbk.)
  6-pack ISBN 978-1-4358-0200-1
  ISBN 978-1-4358-3014-1 (library binding)
  1. Roads—United States—Juvenile literature. I. Title.
  TE149.G69 2009
  388.10973-dc22
                              2008047094

Manufactured in the United States of America

CONTENTS

HIGHWAYS THROUGHOUT HISTORY

A highway is a major public road connecting important locations, especially towns and cities. Today's highways are paved routes used by people driving **motor vehicles**. These roads are governed by rules that all people must follow to avoid confusion and accidents. Governments spend millions of dollars a year making new highways and maintaining the ones that already exist. Countries depend on these **transportation** routes to help support their economies and allow people to travel from one place to another quickly and safely.

Highway interchanges, such as this one, are marvels of modern technology. American highways have come a long way in a short time.

Incan road

Ancient Highways

People have been building and maintaining highways for as long as civilizations have needed to transport people and goods between distant cities. The ancient Romans built stone roads throughout the Roman Empire. This allowed them to move armies, goods, and messages quickly, which helped them expand and unite their empire. The Incas also had a far-reaching series of stone roads along the Pacific Coast of South America. The ancient Roman and Incan highways were not as well governed and maintained as modern highways are. However, some still exist today.

The Rise of the Automobile

In the early 1900s, the best roads in the United States were in cities. The railroad was the main way of traveling long distances. Local roads were usually dirt trails that made travel difficult in bad weather. Some roads were covered with gravel, stone, or brick. These were usually maintained by the people living along them. At the time, most people thought only the wealthy could afford to take long trips on **interstate** roads.

This photo shows a brick-paved street in Midlothian, Illinois, around 1900.

Around 1910, however, the automobile was becoming more popular and affordable. Some Americans, especially leaders of the automobile **industry**, wanted paved public roads to connect towns and cities across America. It wasn't long before a **transcontinental** highway was suggested.

This picture was taken around 1914. It shows a dirt and stone road in Washington State. The motorcycles are stuck in the mud.

CARL G. FISHER

Carl G. Fisher was born in Greensburg, Indiana, on January 12, 1874. In 1891, Fisher and his brothers opened a bicycle repair shop to make money on the bicycle craze that was sweeping the country. By the early 1900s, this fascination with bicycles started to fade and was replaced by a new interest—the automobile. Fisher, who was an enthusiastic bicyclist, became very interested in automobiles and automobile racing. He and a friend

Carl G. Fisher

opened what many believe was the first **car dealership** in America. Fisher became known for staging shows to advertise his products. He once pushed a car off the roof of his car dealership in front of a crowd and then drove it away to prove that it was a dependable product!

After getting injured while car racing, Fisher began supporting the idea of automobile safety. On his advice, the Indianapolis Motor Speedway was paved with bricks to reduce racing accidents. The idea worked, and car racing became safer and more popular. He also wanted to improve the safety features of automobiles. In 1904, Fisher teamed up with an inventor who had a patent for a new car headlight. Together they started the Prest-O-Lite headlight company. Thanks to Fisher's advertising skill, soon almost every car on the road had Prest-O-Lite headlights. This made Fisher a wealthy man, as well as a powerful figure in the automobile industry. His new position would

THE BRICKYARD

Sections of the Indianapolis Motor Speedway were paved with asphalt starting in 1936. By 1961, all but a 3-foot-wide (.9-meter-wide) strip of bricks at the starting line was paved. Today, the Indianapolis Motor Speedway—also known as the Brickyard—is still one of the most popular automobile racetracks in America.

LINCOLN

L

HIGHWAY

eventually help him get the support he needed from other automobile businessmen to launch his most important project.

As the automobile became more popular, automobile owners began taking longer trips. Fisher recognized the need for a safe, hard-surface road across America. He also knew that poor roads would only harm his ability to make money in the automobile industry. He soon came up with the idea for a coast-to-coast hard-surface highway.

Carl G. Fisher was . . .

quality	how we know
good with machines	opened a bicycle repair shop and a car dealership
daring	enjoyed racing bicycles and automobiles
good salesman	staged shows to advertise his products
ambitious	often worked on several projects at the same time
inventive	helped create and sell several original products, including a car headlight
practical	recognized the need for safety features on cars and safer roads
good speaker	convinced many people to help fund the Lincoln Highway
wealthy	made a lot of money selling cars and headlights, and from other projects

Early roads were nothing more than dirt trails. This made travel difficult and sometimes dangerous.

MAKING THE IDEA
A REALITY

Fisher wasn't the first to come up with the idea of a coast-to-coast highway. The U.S. Congress had recently talked about the idea, but they didn't want to pay for it. In September 1912, Fisher held a meeting for the leaders of the automobile industry in Indianapolis, Indiana. Those in attendance included Frank Seiberling of the Goodyear Tire and Rubber Company;

Henry Joy, shown here, was elected president of the association in charge of planning and building the coast-to-coast highway, and Carl Fisher was elected vice president.

Henry Joy, president of the Packard Motor Car Company; and possibly Henry Ford, founder and owner of the Ford Motor Company. Fisher told those present that paving a coast-to-coast highway with concrete would require about $10 million. He called it the "Coast-to-Coast Rock Highway."

The Lincoln Highway Association

Ford was in favor of a highway, but refused to help fund it. He believed that the government, not public or private groups, should build national roads. Seiberling and Joy both promised to give money toward the construction of the highway. Other contributors were inventor Thomas Edison, President Woodrow Wilson, and former president Theodore Roosevelt.

Henry Ford

Frank Seiberling

13

Fisher was a good salesman, and he eventually raised more than $4 million toward the project.

On July 1, 1913, the men announced the formation of an association that would help create a transcontinental highway. Many names were suggested, including the "American Road" and the "Fisher Highway." They decided to honor the sixteenth president of the United States by naming the road the Lincoln Highway. The association became known as the Lincoln Highway Association (LHA).

The "Trail-Blazers"

The next step was to begin planning a route for the highway. Fisher wanted the route to begin in New York City, New York, and end in San Francisco, California. The highway would follow established trails and roads east of the Mississippi River. There weren't many roads west of the Mississippi River, so the LHA needed to send an **expedition** to find and map the

This is one of Henry Joy's Packard automobiles. It was one of the first cars to drive on the Lincoln Highway.

best route west. The group chosen to do this, which included Carl Fisher as its leader, was dramatically named the "Trail-Blazers." A trailblazer is someone who creates, or blazes, a route or path for others to follow.

On July 1, 1913—the same day the formation of the LHA was announced—seventeen cars and two trucks set out from Indianapolis, Indiana, to explore possible routes to San Francisco. The governments of

many cities sent committees to meet the Trail-Blazers, hoping to convince the planners to route the Lincoln Highway through their cities. Some cities even rushed to build sections of road through their towns before the Trail-Blazers arrived, hoping the existence of those roads would help persuade the planners. The LHA decided it was more important to construct the straightest route possible, rather than routing the highway through cities. The expedition reached San Francisco 34 days after leaving Indianapolis.

The trip was difficult at times. The Trail-Blazers had to struggle through deep mud holes and hot desert sand dunes. They sometimes had to carry cars across streams that had no bridges.

PLANNING AND PAVING

On September 14, 1913, the LHA announced an official route for the Lincoln Highway. They had chosen a series of dirt trails and "improved roadways" covered with gravel, stone, brick, or packed sand. Soon after the announcement, the LHA changed the route to make it even straighter. New sections passed by towns like Marion, Ohio, and South Bend, Indiana. Many people, including those who had sent committees to meet the Trail-Blazers in Kansas and Colorado, were upset that the road would not be passing through their states and cities. Denver, Colorado, and other cities planned their own

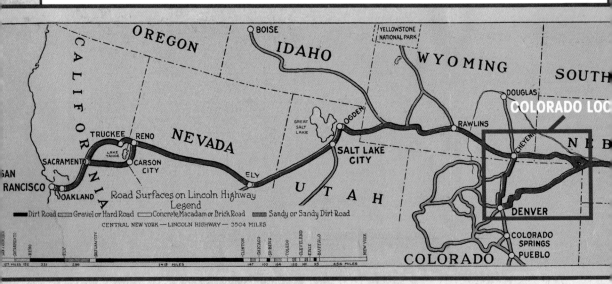

The original route included a "loop" connecting Denver, Colorado, to the Lincoln Highway. The "Colorado Loop" was removed from the route in 1915.

paved roads to connect them to the Lincoln Highway. Many of the cities that were on the final route held parades to celebrate the announcement.

"Seedling Miles"

As word of the highway spread throughout the nation, many people sent **donations** to the LHA to help complete the project. However, Fisher soon realized that they still wouldn't be able to raise enough to pave the entire Lincoln Highway with concrete. The LHA decided to spend their money teaching people about the highway and the future of concrete roads in the United States. To prove that concrete roads were best, short sections of the highway were paved. The government, members of the automobile industry,

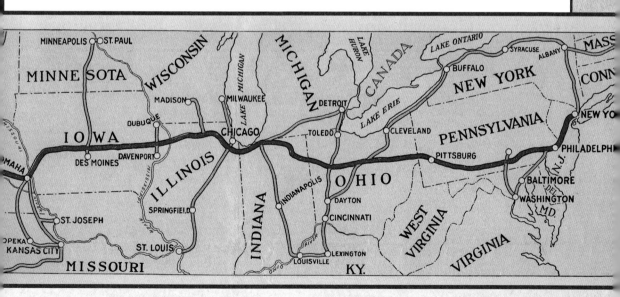

These two photos show a concrete company paving the Ideal Section.

and concrete companies funded these sections, which became known as "seedling miles." They were meant to convince Americans that highways needed to be paved to work properly. The first seedling mile was completed near Malta, Illinois, in the fall of 1914.

LINCOLN
L
HIGHWAY

"THE IDEAL SECTION"

In 1923, the most famous seedling mile was completed in Lake County, Indiana. Known as the "Ideal Section," it was widely advertised in newspapers and magazines as a "vision of the future." It truly was. Highway officials from around the country came to see it and study it. Today, the Ideal Section is still in use.

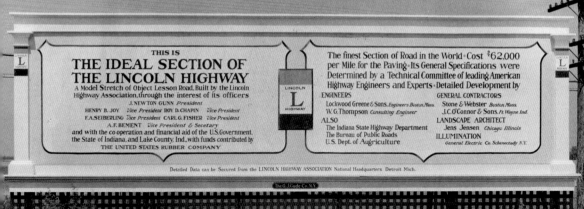

THIS IS
THE IDEAL SECTION OF
THE LINCOLN HIGHWAY
A Model Stretch of Object Lesson Road, Built by the Lincoln Highway Association, through the interest of its officers
J. NEWTON GUNN *President*
HENRY B. JOY *Vice President* ROY D. CHAPIN *Vice President*
F.A. SEIBERLING *Vice President* CARL G. FISHER *Vice President*
A.F. BEMENT *Vice President & Secetary*
and with the co operation and financial aid of the U.S. Government, the State of Indiana, and Lake County, Ind., with funds contributed by
THE UNITED STATES RUBBER COMPANY

LINCOLN
L
HIGHWAY

The finest Section of Road in the World · Cost $62,000 per Mile for the Paving · Its General Specifications were Determined by a Technical Committee of leading American Highway Engineers and Experts · Detailed Development by
ENGINEERS
Lockwood Greene & Sons. *Engineers Boston, Mass.*
W. G. Thompson *Consulting Engineer*
ALSO
The Indiana State Highway Department
The Bureau of Public Roads
U.S. Dept. of Agriculture
GENERAL CONTRACTORS
Stone & Webster *Boston Mass.*
J.C. O'Connor & Sons. *Ft. Wayne Ind.*
LANDSCAPE ARCHITECT
Jens Jensen *Chicago Illinois*
ILLUMINATION
General Electric Co. Schenectady N.Y.

Detailed Data can be Secured from the LINCOLN HIGHWAY ASSOCIATION National Headquarters Detroit Mich.

The O.J.Gude Co. N.Y.

AMERICA'S RESPONSE TO THE LINCOLN HIGHWAY

The announcement of the route for the Lincoln Highway caused a lot of enthusiasm across the country. However, the highway was not completed as quickly as Fisher had hoped it would be. For years, it remained a series of freshly paved highways and unpaved dirt trails. According to an early guidebook to the Lincoln Highway, the idea of driving the entire route was "something of a sporting **proposition**." The guidebook recommended that drivers bring special supplies, including shovels, axes, **car jacks**, water, new tires, and camping supplies. The guidebook also said travelers should not wear new shoes!

Testing the Lincoln Highway

In 1919, the U.S. military tested the Lincoln Highway by shipping goods from Washington, D.C., to San Francisco. The **convoy**, made up of

U.S. military convoy on the Lincoln Highway

Driving on the Lincoln Highway was often hard. This picture, taken in 1915, shows a car stuck in deep mud after a rainstorm.

seventy-five trucks, broke eighty-eight bridges along the way! The trucks often became stuck in deep mud. This helped convince the U.S. government that the country needed better roads and bridges.

"Main Street Across America"

Despite the early difficulties, the Lincoln Highway quickly gained support. The new coast-to-coast highway had a positive effect on the growing country. Businesses in towns and cities along the route grew quickly as new customers drove by the shops, restaurants, hotels, gas stations, and garages. Many small towns grew into cities thanks to the Lincoln Highway. Soon people were calling it the "Main Street Across America."

Once the federal government started funding road projects, the LHA finally established a fixed route for the highway. They were also able to pave large sections with concrete. Notice the old section of dirt road on the left.

Each year, the Lincoln Highway was improved and rerouted to make it more **efficient**. Throughout the 1920s, the highway became a place to test new ways of paving and bridge building. The highway's original route was paved by 1938. By that time, state governments had seen the importance of paved highways, and new roads were being planned and built all over the country.

PAVING AMERICA

Due to the success of the Lincoln Highway, other public groups began to plan their own interstate highways. In 1914, Fisher helped to organize the building of the Dixie Highway system from Michigan to Florida. The Jefferson Highway stretched from New Orleans, Louisiana, to Winnipeg, Canada. In 1925, the federal government began using numbers to identify highways. Most sections of the Lincoln Highway were relabeled with numbers, and many of these route numbers are still used today.

Dwight Eisenhower

In 1956, President Dwight D. Eisenhower—who had been part of the military convoy that tested the Lincoln Highway in 1919—helped pass the Federal-Aid Highway Act. The act provided $25 billion for the construction of 41,000 miles (65,969 km) of interstate highway over a 20-year period. Eisenhower argued that modern highways were necessary for effective national defense. If the country were ever attacked, he argued, the military would need strong roads and bridges to make travel quick and easy.

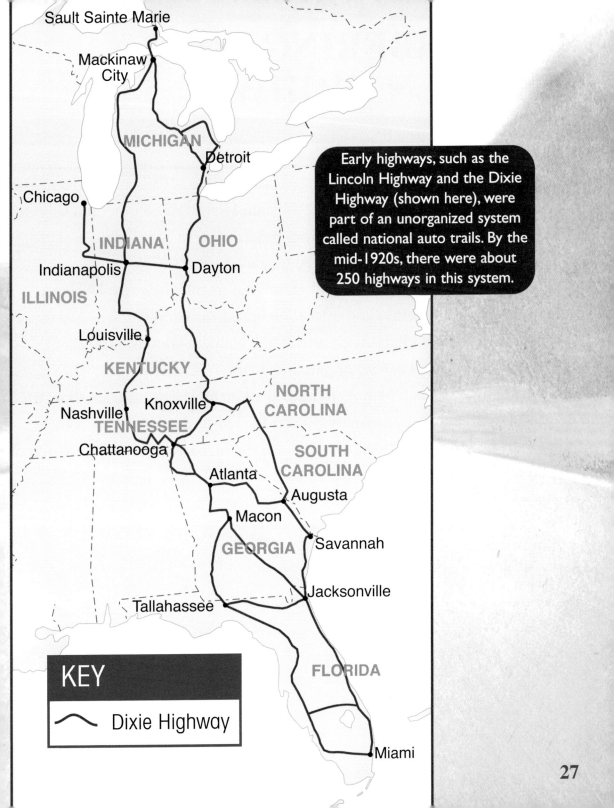

Sault Sainte Marie

Mackinaw City

MICHIGAN

Detroit

Chicago

INDIANA   OHIO

Indianapolis   Dayton

ILLINOIS

Louisville

KENTUCKY

Knoxville   NORTH CAROLINA

Nashville
TENNESSEE

Chattanooga   SOUTH CAROLINA

Atlanta

Augusta

Macon

Savannah

GEORGIA

Jacksonville

Tallahassee

FLORIDA

Early highways, such as the Lincoln Highway and the Dixie Highway (shown here), were part of an unorganized system called national auto trails. By the mid-1920s, there were about 250 highways in this system.

KEY

Dixie Highway

Miami

REMEMBERING THE LINCOLN HIGHWAY

The LHA officially ended in 1927, but it had left a lasting influence on the United States. The success of the Lincoln Highway and other publicly funded highways convinced the federal government to connect more of America's towns and cities with paved highways.

By the 1950s, the Lincoln Highway was nearly forgotten. Modern, federally funded highways and interstates linked the nation's towns and cities. Today, the National Highway System in the United States includes about 160,000 miles (257,440 km) of paved highways.

Starting in the 1990s, sections of the Lincoln Highway were recognized as historic places. Many stretches are **scenic** roads today. The LHA, which started up again in 1992, helps to preserve the highway. Without the vision of Carl G. Fisher and the LHA, who knows what America's highways would be like today?

cause:
The LHA announces the route of the Lincoln Highway.

effect: Upset that the road wouldn't be passing through their states, some cities planned their own paved roads to connect them to the Lincoln Highway.

effect: Many people and businesses sent donations to the LHA.

effect: Other public groups began to plan and build their own interstate highways.

effect: The money helped fund seedling miles such as the Ideal Section.

effect: Seedling miles helped demonstrate that concrete roads are better than dirt roads.

effect: The U.S. military tested the road with a convoy of seventy-five trucks.

effect: Businesses in towns and cities along the route grew quickly.

effect: The convoy frequently got stuck in deep mud and broke eighty-eight bridges along the route.

effect: Many small towns grew into cities.

effect: U.S. government began to understand the need for paved roads and better bridges.

effect: People started calling the Lincoln Highway the "Main Street Across America."

29

LINCOLN L HIGHWAY

January 12, 1874 Carl G. Fisher is born.

Around 1900 The automobile begins to grow in popularity in the United States. Fisher opens what many believe was the first car dealership.

September 1912 Fisher holds a meeting for leaders of the automobile industry to discuss a coast-to-coast highway.

July 1, 1913 Fisher announces the formation of the Lincoln Highway Association. The Trail-Blazers set out from Indianapolis and arrive in San Francisco 34 days later.

September 14, 1913 The LHA announces the official route of the Lincoln Highway.

1914 The first seedling mile is completed near Malta, Illinois.

1919 The U.S. military tests the Lincoln Highway with a convoy of seventy-five trucks.

1923 The Ideal Section is completed in Lake County, Indiana.

1925 The federal government begins using numbers to identify highways.

1927 The LHA officially ends.

1938 The original route is paved with concrete.

1956 President Dwight D. Eisenhower helps pass the Federal-Aid Highway Act.

1992 The LHA starts up again.

GLOSSARY

car dealership (KAHR DEE-luhr-ship) A place where cars are sold.

car jack (KAHR JAK) A tool used to raise one side of a car into the air so a tire can be changed.

convoy (KAHN-voi) A group of cars or trucks traveling together.

donation (doh-NAY-shun) A gift of money or help.

efficient (ih-FIH-shunt) Functioning in the quickest or best way possible.

expedition (ehk-spuh-DIH-shun) A trip made by a group of people to explore unknown territory, or the people who go on the trip.

industry (IHN-duhs-tree) A collective term for all the businesses in a field.

interstate (IHN-tuhr-stayt) A federally funded highway that connects major U.S. cities.

motor vehicle (MOH-tuhr VEE-uh-kuhl) A car, truck, or other motorized form of transportation.

proposition (prah-puh-ZIH-shun) An idea put forward for consideration or discussion.

scenic (SEE-nihk) Traveling through beautiful natural areas.

transcontinental (trans-kahn-tuh-NEHN-tuhl) Going across a continent.

transportation (trans-puhr-TAY-shun) A way of traveling from one place to another.

INDEX

C

coast-to-coast, 10, 12, 13, 24, 30
concrete, 13, 19, 21, 29, 30
convoy, 22, 26, 29, 30

D

Dixie Highway, 26

E

Edison, Thomas, 13
Eisenhower, President Dwight D., 26, 30

F

Federal-Aid Highway Act, 26, 30
Fisher, Carl G., 8, 9, 10, 12, 13, 14, 15, 19, 22, 26, 28, 30
Ford, Henry, 13

H

headlight(s), 9, 10

I

Ideal Section, 21, 29, 30
Incas, 5

Indianapolis, Indiana, 12, 15, 16, 30
Indianapolis Motor Speedway, 8, 9
interstate(s), 6, 26, 28, 29

J

Jefferson Highway, 26
Joy, Henry, 13

L

Lake County, Indiana, 21, 30
Lincoln Highway Association (LHA), 14, 15, 16, 18, 19, 28, 29, 30

M

"Main Street Across America," 24, 29
Malta, Illinois, 21, 30

N

National Highway System, 28
New York City, New York, 14

P

pave(d), 4, 6, 8, 9, 19, 21, 22, 25, 28, 29, 30
Prest-O-Lite, 9

R

Roman(s), 5, 6
Roosevelt, Theodore, 13

S

San Francisco, California, 14, 15, 16, 22, 30
seedling mile(s), 21, 29, 30
Seiberling, Frank, 12, 13

T

Trail-Blazers, 15, 16, 18, 30
transcontinental, 6, 14

W

Washington, D.C., 22
Wilson, President Woodrow, 13